T0083449

THE STORM

AND OTHER POEMS

THE
STORM

AND OTHER POEMS

William Pitt Root

Carnegie Mellon University Press
Pittsburgh 2005

Library of Congress Control Number: 2005920798
ISBN 0-88748-444-1
Copyright © 1968 by William Pitt Root
All rights reserved
Printed and bound in the United States of America
First Carnegie Mellon University Press Edition, 2005

10 9 8 7 6 5 4 3 2 1

The Storm and Other Poems was first published by
Atheneum in 1968

Many of these poems have appeared previously in the following
periodicals, magazines, and anthologies: THE ATLANTIC MONTHLY, BELOIT
POETRY JOURNAL, CAROLINA QUARTERLY, THE CATALYST, CORADDI, THE
GREENSBORO READER, THE GREENSBORO REVIEW, HUDSON REVIEW, MASSACHUSETTS
REVIEW, THE NATION, NORTHWEST REVIEW, THE NOW READER FOR THE NOW
WRITER, POETRY NORTHWEST, PRAIRIE SCHOONER, RED CEDAR REVIEW, RED CLAY
READER 3, RED CLAY READER 5, SEWANEE REVIEW, SHENANDOAH, SOUTHERN
POETRY REVIEW (formerly IMPETUS), TRACE, VIRGINIA QUARTERLY REVIEW,
WEST COAST REVIEW, YANKEE.

The publisher expresses gratitude to David Harmon
and Pat Martinak, Alkahest Bookshop, Deerfield,
Illinois for assistance in producing this volume.

Thanks are due as well to James Reiss and
James W. Hall for their ongoing contributions to the
Classic Contemporaries Series.

This book is for my wife and daughter,
my mother and sisters and the memory of my father,
for friends, who have taught me and whom I love,
for teachers, who have been my friends.

Contents

I

THE DREAM

I dreamt that I would die
and could not wake. A space
of darkness, viscid, warm,
engulfed me—I floated. A fold

of fire split the dark,
gave vision, spilled
a shallow light that burned,
burned as I felt it flood

the swollen rim, and heard
a cry, then watched it issue
smoke and ash and fire.
It closed. I dreamt I woke.

II

WHISKEY CREEK BRIDGE

Standing on the wooden bridge at Whiskey Creek
where my father's old and new farms join,
I listen for a moment: everything is silent
save mosquitoes and the stiff dry-sounding dragonflies
that skim the water's smooth back for dark specks.

Below me, poised and waiting
in silver webs that flex under the bridge,
huge spiders shine and dangle in the dark,
the harmlessly exotic and the deadly,
a black widow looming by the dry shell of her mate,
her womb filled with seed fed by its father's flesh,
the hourglass of blood set in her belly.

Where water clear as amber runs,
I watch the sluggish traffic from the swamps
drain toward the Gulf: cypress branches wrapped in moss,
    half sunk,
rigid garfish, mullet in dull swarms, cottonmouths and perch,
broad leaves turning slowly in the underwater light
and a variety of turtles—some soft-shelled and graceful,
some with brilliant faces, orange and yellow streaked
as if their budshaped heads were splitting into bloom,
and some, harder, darker, whose horned beaks crack
the other's shells and ream them while they die—,
all moving downstream to feed the broad Caloosahatchee

where fresh water and salt collide and mingle,
where seabirds, sand sharks and bull gators wait.

When a branch snaps and falls, breaking the surface,
I start with the fish, shivers of rising silver
that feign and turn, vanish into the spreading calm
where the shadow of my childhood holds them all,
a darkness deep almost beyond my seeing.

THE WAVERING FIELD

The plow has stunned the farmer's hands with callous.
Waiting for the boy, he attempts to balance
his body's exhaustion with the land's. From above
the sun's oceanic glare discovers
the wavering field, where seeds root in the waste
of crops plowed under. He runs with sweat,
his face and raised arm gleam. Both feet
hidden in the broken earth, he leans
against the stock and shades his eyes—his legs
a clay of sweat and dust smoked from the acres
his plow has cut—to watch his youngest son,
real against the shimmering horizon,
run from the house and past the family graveyard.
A mason jar of water shines in his arms.

FIELD LATE IN THE FALL

The dry sleeves of the corn stalks
flap and rattle, alive with gestures
of wind, as the wired black feet
of the glistening crows hold fast.

Bobbing and swaying on hollow spines,
they bow when the stalks are bowed by wind
that whines in their black empty beaks.
Their eyes glitter with ants and beetles.

Above them, the living call and wheel.

THE GULF

How they burn,
the manes of his horses
in the light-torn
waves, like curses

in an ancient dream,
a Viking sailor's
nightmare, brim
with serpents, failures.

From the cliff
the father shouts.
He shouts again,

and hears a laugh
as the surf shifts,
surrounding his son.

ON THE TIDAL LEDGE

Near a headland
while I closed my eyes and listened,
I heard them cry, drowning, in the wind.
I looked, and the illusion disappeared.
They hovered bright above the waves
where cresting edges shattered
on gusts of wind the sky alone imagined
while I watched.

Excited, but cold,
I hunched a bit and moved on toward a cove
where the tidal ledge is pocked
with cup- and basin-sized pools.
I found a ringed anemone
open in a vulgar bulge of moss on a rock.

Curious with an idle kind of jealousy,
malicious,
I teased the ancient total mouth
with little stones.
Wiser than I'd known
the anemone ignored the bait of pebbles,
then closed around my finger
sinking shut against its stone. I felt it
fix its tiny hooks.
My finger stung, I jerked it free.
The flesh had barely tingled,
but I was tight with dread

at how cold seaflesh is
and how it feels: It clings like a kiss.

I watched the soft jawbelly
dilating slowly
on its deep bald face of stone,
the cilia, like eyelashes, wavering
with hunger on their round blind lid.
Swollen wide, it spilled out grains of sand
that tumbled toward a growing pile
already at the bottom of the pool.

I moved beyond decaying stone
and trapped water, its creature.
                            I left it
waiting at the temperature of death, and tried
to find again wings and eyes shining
in a knowledge of the light.

PASSING A SAWMILL AT NIGHT

The road was straight. A gully braced by stumps
plunged from the edge. Beyond it, a fall field
widened through the darkness toward a clump
of trees in silhouette against the sawmill wall.
Slowing down, I watched the bright smoke's
scattered ashes dying among stars.

Years before, without a word spoken,
my father stopped the jeep as we hunted his farm.
Our years together ending, the stubble behind us bright
with frost, we watched a distant mill's dark walls
pulse with swollen squares of fire. "At night,"
he had told me (he still moves through the smells
of oil and gunpowder, night itself,
reaching to release the brake), "we know
more than we can learn of death, and life."

I stopped the car slowly. My wife leaned
against my arm, asleep. Across the road,
through the living trees, the taken burned.

THE PASSAGE OF THE LIVING

VESPERS

As a train in the night gains speed,
I wake to darkness, think of light
careering through frail galaxies
of frosted wire and weeds that
glitter and vanish in fields
beyond the town, and farther still
through foothills and the dark passes
blasted from their darker stone
that dangerously lean
against the passage of the living
through the darkness, through the sleep
of children dreaming, men and women dreaming
as the dark cries to their dreams
and their dreams cry back.

MATINS

Now the starlit dew burns on the branch
and spins the tree, spins the rooted earth
in planet light, and falls. Brightness burns
the angled stones, consumes the darkness ripe
within the yawing trunks and radiant underleaves.
Dawn burns and the creatures wake
from desperate sleep, and stare.

III

A DREAM OF SNOW

At the Zoo After a Visit to the Clinic

Trembling, as if with joy,
palsied in her shining chair,
the girl confronts the beasts that turn
and turn before each cage to stare.

Once long cages braced the legs
now brightly hidden in soft wools,
and from those early secret nights
when, innocent, she'd study how her muscles
dwindled till she slept,
she still remembers tingling tigers
creeping through her flesh in darkness,
stalking men of sticks and ice
in dreams of cold, dreams of snow.

Now the back-and-shoulder jungle parts
and brightens: a leopard's stare
blocks the bars. His urine-yellow eyes
alert, sharpened by her helplessness,
stir her with their hopeless, deadly sympathy.

CEREMONY

Deep in the calm of a drawing room of flowers
the only hand her father holds
is dead.

       Years ago,
behind a locked and broken bathroom door,
they found a man with eyes of dull blue silk
hanging from a tie stretched thin and knotted
in his puckered throat.
              She felt her father's love
as in a shock of tenderness, his hand quickened
her arm, and loosened, dropped away. She left
them kneeling, one still, one slowly
turning, head cocked, hands loosely bound
and naked in a small bright room,—her father
in the slowly turning shadow of his son.

She sits apart, alone
in the alcove reserved for close relations.
Staring through the arch that frames
her mother's face and brother's
in her memory, she knows that if her father sees
he sees her framed in that same arch of flowers,
watching, heart and buttocks clenched
as at his touch.
       Among the heads before her
she sees a former suitor's dull profile,
his wife, her father's business partner
and a friend, then half a dozen friends,

a row of strangers who look up to turn away.
She knows the faces dark with memories
she cannot know, and watches each face
patterned by the shadow of its neighbor,
watches features vanish, then reappear as restlessness
shifts a wife or husband, or a stranger
turns to stare and look away.
He is gone now,
he is gone, and who are you to sit prim
among roses and lilies, breathing
this sweet stench of bright dead flowers,
breathing? Now he's gone: without him,
who are you? Breathing among roses,
half-opened and dead, breathing
among lilies and roses, who are you?

he is gone now

he is gone   please now   he is gone
the grass is soft   and look   the house
is empty   we're alone now   please

the grass is soft

the grass is soft and

he is gone now

please the grass is soft the grass
is soft the grass is soft

with hands and

please the grass is

blue eyes

please

dull blue

please

Please

Please! she cries,

and sees them turn to stare. The blank profile
turns and starts to rise, a stranger, a frightened face
that says familiar words. On everyone
his neighbor's shadow falls.
                              Outside,
the sun is green in summer leaves and grass.
She sees his boy, a face pressed to the glass,
as he stares from the car at their approach. They enter,
sit in silence, and watch the child run to his mother.
Passing cars flash the sun's sharp light
against their faces.
                    Are you all right?,
he asks. She nods an answer,
takes the hand he gives,
then lets him lead her to the waiting grave.

THE DEATH OF A FAMILY

The feral boys in Sunday suits
can scarcely be distinguished
from the grey branches they seize,
rattling them to fling the pecans down.

Their fathers are below them, gathering
what falls; they are motions anxious
in fallen leaves the patriarch despises,
but will not rake away.

At twilight in his wasting house,
the women—intimidated by relief,
regret, and willful love—surround him,
imploring eyes fervid with decay.

Above them all, below them,
moonlight and dry frozen roots spread
and clutch, contending for a world beyond
the coins and curtains of his tended sleep.

RETREAT NEAR MT. TAMALPAIS, CALIFORNIA

Searchers were unable to locate the driver's body although at one point it was believed blood had been discovered leading from the wreckage at the bottom of the cliff into woods toward a distant monastery.

There is a place, a valley
dropping through hills
toward the sea,

where a man—whose body
spills, whose twilit eyes brim
with the shadows of Sequoias—

is allowed to hear vespers
as if at a great distance
whispered from assembled stones

cold atop a hill and dim
with candles: this
in the impulse of a dumb

maggot furious
at the base of his tongue.

ONE SUNDAY

A Grandfather's Tale

One Sunday, when the quick rain fell,
what happened by a scarcely dampened dusty road
on grass still dry under an oak
is that they heard the restless bay mare
snort and stamp, jangling her harness
where their buggy stood in silence, halfway home,
and I was born in earshot of the next spring's Sunday bells.

THE GRANDFATHER

From wave to wave a flat rock skips,
skids. An edge catches. It flips and sinks.
Each time he throws, the watch in his pocket clinks

on the coins and collected pebbles. How many trips
he's made back here, to pry stones from their chinks.
    From wave to wave each flat rock skips,
    skids till it catches an edge, flips, and sinks.

His wife complains, insists that his pocket rips
from carrying "sharp, dirty stones." She thinks
aloud, "He's my oldest child." Their grandson blinks.
    From wave to wave the flat rock skips,
    skids. When it catches its edge, flips and sinks,
      the water twinkles. He flinches. The watch in his pocket
      clinks.

TOWARD NIGHT AN OLD MAN
DROVE TO SEARCH

for rotted firewood. He'd started late
and from a hill above the darkened curve
where coastlands hunch along the sea, he made

uncertain guesses at where the house he lived in
stood. A closing lid of fog had changed
the ocean to a rumpled field of vivid

silent clouds. And as the coastland's shape
surrendered, on the hill he carried sticks
and crumbling, fungus-covered logs, laid

them in his trunk, then slammed it shut. At peace
he coasted down the road. The sun had faded
like an aging eye. He couldn't see

—with lights or without—and all the way
he breathed the wood's narcotic, ripe decay.

ACCIDENT ON THE HIGHWAY
AT NIGHT

His mind smears with stars.
Numb, his body is the earth
spilling on itself. Then
eyes: moving mouths: faces flashing
blood. Swaying, the far clear moon.

AUGUST AT SIXTY

For Gail

She stands alone now, widowed in their garden
with the comfort of his roses
hung from ruined stems.
The mannered children, who were kind, are gone,
resuming lives remote from her again.

She plucks off yellow leaves and ties up stalks
the dry weather has weakened.
Her apron fills with leaves.
Stiff fingers brush her belly, breasts and hair,
trembling with this new life she must bear.

THE END OF WINTER
IN AN OLD NEIGHBORHOOD

I

    Today is not quite spring
    but now the Marchlit windows
    widen,
        show the screen
    of thin dry twigs that flinch
    as sparrows hop.

      Cracking buds
perch
like beetles split
       for flight:
          gables jut,
              bay windows
            belly out against the wind.

This neighborhood of ancient rooms
      pulses
        as creatures flock,
disband
and come again,
        one by one,
          to fill the twitching branches,
          the empty sunlit rooms.

A green vine flares along the twigs
    steady on its amber claws

                                    and as the branches heave
      the hook tips catch:
                          it rides.

                          The seasons
                    tremble everywhere.

2

      Today from Minnesota came a letter
      from grandmother:

      "Bright storms raged around us
but they missed us and we have
                          a lovely sunday morning
nice and cool
                    though saddened by the stroke a patient had
last night she lost her voice and cannot move
her eyes

      "My boy you'd see my second childhood
if you could see me now   I crawl along in bed
quite on my own
                          and in my infant fashion am quite free
            I feel
so free
            after these months stiffened in
traction and ridiculous in casts
we even have some fun

      "The wind changes direction
often so the nurses run   opening and closing
windows asking how we feel   too warm too cool
                                    too late
to write much more now
I must nap

"And now we've had our evening meal   one
hears the cart that clatters like so many bones
and pauses
                and the opening and closing
of the doors to all the rooms as it passes   stops in silence
starts moving room by room along the hall
                                        at the end
                it waits for us
to finish
                then the clatter once again
of glass on hard white steel

        "They say my bones are hardening again
like sponge they were   so soft I couldn't stand
                                        they wouldn't
hold my body up   I weigh just ninety-five now like I did when
I was twenty and all day long
                        I wear a nightie   this one or
another but they're laundered here so often that they fade
bleached without light
                        and how I miss the color
                of my hair
        'scarlet mane' your mother called it
    and your father 'burning bush'
so short now   they keep it
cut so short

        "It's good to be in bed
with the moonlight on the snow
                                two pillows prop my head
and the snow is like a sheet that wraps the world   the room
is rather dim   the other patients sleep
                                and I must close

or I will wake and think this letter was a dream
and write again and say this all again
but I can feel our winter's
nearly over"

FISHERMAN

A woman comes
to watch her lover pull nets from the sea.

His back bulges with ocean waves
contenting her a moment while his body,
black against the sun,
is swollen with such power
the slow dull sea around him trembles light.

She drops to her knees
and waits with sealight blowing in her hair
and with her skirt
she shades what she has brought.

Noon.

He sees her, shrugs the stone-gleam of his shoulder
and drags the living weight up onto land,
each wave trying to drag it back.

He joins her in dry grass beyond the sand.

Wine from a bottle tall and cool
in its wrapping of wet rags, a loaf,
a wedge of cheese, an apple and a knife.

While sunlight plays on dying fish
in thrashing brilliance

he chews and sees her eyes darken for him
and he is glad and laughs.

They are young
and neither seems to notice
the distant net
flashing,

the frantic sound of a thousand fingers snapping.

A pale gull slowly wheels a relic circle,
then is gone.

IV

THE FIRSTBORN

Our first child
  was early, "easy"
they told her, and telling me
  she smiled,
pretended to smile. The pillow case
was white, the sheet-stains hidden, her face

familiar, strange.
  And full of guilt
beyond delivery, I felt
  as strange
as Adam joining Eve, feigning pride
while I brought her a rose bright as blood.

THE VISITING HOUR

For Judy

As I drove the road I raced the night before,
my headlights' steady glaring hid the stars.
They weren't yet sure our seven-month daughter
could live. I'd known her first night, her horror

muffled by the glass room and Isolette,
the crescent bruises where forceps took her face.
I smoked as I drove, smelling the room where I'd waited,
its shallow cactus of dead cigarettes,

the insurance man whose daughter wouldn't breathe.
I was leaning against a curve when I saw the eyes.
I braked and swerved but felt the thud and cry
before I could stop. I looked, and found a piece

of bleeding fur, wedged in the front bumper.
The bright racoon was gone; dead, or perhaps
—stunned and hidden in the roadside grass—
waiting till I left to move, or whimper.

Where headlights turned the trunks of trees to stone,
I made my frightened search through weeds. I knew
the racoon lived; but only shadows moved
as I passed the dark curve later, driving home.

LIVING IT UP,

While the Wife Is with Her Folks

I hear my watch ticking in the June grass
as my dog leans its head against a fast
thumping foot, and then rolls over.
Paper-littered waves slop below
our dock, and splattered brace-planks gleam.

The blonde who rents next door seems
to wave as she cleans her picture window,
using a sponge and a rubber glove that's yellow.
I feel I could wave back, so I stare
as she polishes the glass. However, finished there,

she moves from sight to a window on the side.
Behind a corner of the house her body hides
as her busy arm wipes on, detached. And when a
sparrow twitters from her T-V antenna,
the dog whimpers, gnawing at another flea.

A dog's life, I mutter, and turn to see
a runabout riding on a crown of white water.
The crowd aboard is sporting all the colors
of the flag that flaps on the stern above the wake.
The people in it wave. Finally I wave back,

and listen to the ticking June grass.

THE JELLYFISH

There isn't much a man can do
about a grounded jellyfish
except step over it, or prod
it with his walking stick, and if
he has no walking stick, his shoe.
My feet were bare, so I leaned
to watch the waves relax around
the shiny melted-looking heap.

The jellyfish didn't move,
but then, of course, jellyfishes
don't. They navigate at best
like bottles: When the tide shifts
they bob and drift away. But who
has ever seen a living creature
with a note inside?
                              I found
an iridescent fish, uneaten
and twitching still, inside the gluey
drying bowel. I saw it jerk,
expand its gills, then quiver, arrested
loosely, loosely and forever.
It shone with pink and green, blue
and yellow, flashed profoundly silver
in each spasm. I knew it was dead
already, and only seemed to work
to free itself.
                              As I tried to remove
the notion from my mind, the mound

it moved in, like a glassy brain,
was taken from me by a wave
that slid from the ocean without a sound.

HOLOCAUST

The burning church shuddered. In the mire of its light,
the steeple tumbled. A loosened bell broke
the altar into sparks as stained glass windows
burst. Afterward, sorting through the bright
shards of mosaic stories for Moses' burning
bush, I found an infant Christ whose face
was blank with melted lead. The whole place
stank of scalded ash.
     A month of spring
conjured the fire of flowers from shrubs scarred
by the blaze. Some stiff, fire-scalded leaves
were dead, black on top and pale underneath,
but half-bushes bloomed. And now, charred
twigs kink toward the church's shell
while blossoms nod like innocents near hell.

END OF A SEASON

As hot light drinks the puddles
from concrete, and gladiolus
rise like knuckled sticks, God's
day, Sunday, burns. The clouds have opened

just enough, and sunlight stares
the shadows into trees. From bushes,
small birds flip through the air,
or peck at thorns bright with bugs,

feeding where branches are open coffins.
On the lawn a mat of cut
grass rots. A shabby robin
yanks a worm that stretches as he tugs.

It snaps. The gladiolus rattle
if you're close enough to hear,
and there's a breeze. Ants and beetles
crawl along the leaves like paper.

Of three stalks, two are ragged
with dead flowers. The third is tight
with buds, but dry and almost dead
despite the rain, the gardener, and the light.

SNOW

involves
irrelevance,
assumes forms *a priori*
  stone, tree,
  mountainside,

orders
the chaos
visible on slopes or
  fields and, falling,
  softens all

in light,
softens all
the hard dark necessary
  ledge of rock
  wound to the peak

and twigs
that branch down
through clenched earth,
  conceals and shines around
  the informed edge, the hazard.

STARLINGS

Like cones that screech they fill the barren trees.
They think it's spring. I've seen them huddle, huge
with snow-clogged feathers, on withered vines outside
our bedroom window. I heard them late one night,
and rose to watch the whirling dark alone.
They think it's spring. A thaw exposes garbage
in dirt-pitted banks of snow that waste to molds
and curves of sensuous ice. I hold the marriage
ring my flesh has warmed, its weight, and hear,
mid-winter, starlings sing that starve.

IN LATE WINTER

In late winter, when stone-colored trees
steep longer in the tilting light—not yet green
as nuthard buds bundle-in unseen March red,
orange and yellow, bunches brightly locked
and swollen into nubs like toned Indian corn,
not ripe, but ripening—I am drawn toward
water.
        On the dock I walk while dust shakes
from sun-loosened boards. No one comes
while winter stuns the lake with rain.
Fallen specks, locked on water, float
indented into dimples such as needle-footed
insects prick in stepping the taut water's skin.
While the dust disappears, I bend and kneel,
looking through the face the surface juggles.

WHILE THE OCEAN TURNS

I see
their long, thin stems

> —straighter than the white ribs
> of a perch
> sea-snails
> have partially devoured
> on a shelf-rock near the tide—

the thin, green
stems themselves
rising to my shoulder's height,
the fork of blooms widened
from the flower's green,
narrow brain,

> and know

> > the waves are taking
> > rotten flakes
> > like blossoms
> > from the perch's side

> while Queen Anne's Lace
> illuminates the hill, conceals
> the sudden prospect of the cliff,
> consumes me.

THE CITY DREAMING OF HORSES

Each dawn we watch the bus descend
through lifting mist, come shining down
an emerging hill's decline to the sea.
We mount its trembling steps, feed
the chattering meter quarters, sit,
begin to sleep—but first sway round
our tightly curved tidal bay,
begin the lifting road up through
the hillside pastures, passing every
day the dewdrenched buckskin mare
who comes to lean against the leaning
fence and stare as, from our serial
windows, we stare back before we
enter the city dreaming of horses.

SILHOUETTES

In one of the nation's culture-minded cities
—and quite likely in several dozen more—
wait semi-transients, patient human remnants
who gather every morning by the score
in a union hiring hall. Against the wall
where cracked plaster discloses the mean ribs
of lath, they sit on benches. The papers call
these separate men "the labor pool that gives
our state potential."
                    Slouched, they wait and read
the latest news. "The war'll help," says one.
When the others grumble, ashamed, he shakes his head.
"It's true," he says, and stares . . . Against the sun-
lit skylight, a relic from the building's past,
the rain-dropped tadpoles are still, sperm-like, and black.

MALFUNCTION

"At my age, an unimportant spasm.
The heart's a sturdy organ, very strong.
They tell me it's no more than that,

"and who am I to argue? I'm not fat,
not nervous. I'm used to working all day long.
At my age, an unimportant spasm

"—dizziness, momentary lapses.
They know their diagnosis can be wrong.
They tell me it's no more than that

" 'malfunction,' the skipped beat. A fact
to know but not to worry over. Not for long.
At any age, an unimportant spasm

"—dwelt on—can result in the attack.
The heart's a sturdy organ, very strong
they tell me. It's no more than that:

"Strong and sturdy, leaking like a sack.
Each beat more life gone.
At my age, an unimportant spasm.
To tell me it's no more than that!"

LUNCH HOUR

Behind a department store
whose glassy face displays on Market Street,
a one-way alley stretches
a block at a time through the city. Out of sight
and mind, with butts and wine,
it's here the morning drunks slump as papers
blown from refuse boxes
scrape along the asphalt, stiff as crabs.

Because it's quieter here
in the corridor of red brick walls
like cliffs, I sometimes eat
propped against a knobby fire-plug's stump
on the curb. In the sun,
the men around watch as I wad up the sack,
toss it onto the street.
While it crawls along in the wind, I sit with the others
empty-handed. Hunched
like men at a beach, we listen and watch. We wait.

STOCKROOM

The stockroom fills with clocks at noon
—thank God they don't come wound. Until
my time has come, I'll work balloons,
I'll sort deflated faces. Tell
me what they'll mean—a child's puffing
swollen face, his tears, a mother's
breath, his joy, another thing
the wind can pop on thorns, another
thing? I'll sort and count and stack
or hang brassieres and blouses, trusses,
knee-length socks, keeping track
of tennis rackets while the busses
murmur past nine floors
down.
          Once I dropped and broke
a bottle of cologne. Whores,
genie-like, appeared from smoke
no eye could see, no nose ignore.
Dizzily I kneeled to dam
the spreading stain with rags. "More
pantie girdles," wheezed the man
from lingerie. "But these are all
there are," I said, pointing beyond
the toys, cosmetics and dresses for fall
to garments stacked on the pricer's bench.
They glistened like skinned fish.
He winced and, turning from my stench,

he moaned, "There must be more than this,
there must be more than this."
                                At noon,
poised on the window's tilting ledge, I ate
my lunch, repeating with the cadence
of a clock's neat tick:
there must   there must   be more   than this

EXORCISM

In my fever I would dream, remember
nothing of the dream but darkness, heat.
And in my fear and darkness, I kept a candle
by my bed, and watched the shadows pulsing
till I slept and dreamed of darkness, heat.
Finally, on the last night, a fly woke
as I lay and tossed in the flickering dark.
I listened to it tick against the walls,
whir in the air, discovering limits
it neither remembered nor understood
as it ticked against the walls, whirred,
and I tossed, pulsing in my heat.
I slept, but woke to hear the candle
sputter with dry sudden wings.
The flame crouched, then leapt, widened at the base
and steadied while the room stank of singed air.
I woke in the morning cool, dreamless, diminished.

VI

A YEAR HAS PASSED ALREADY, SO

For Tim

Sidestepping the amenities, we leave our wives
awkward with each other in the house,
and balancing our glasses of bright wine,
settle as if forever into a frail pair of lawnchairs
that creak and lean and threaten to collapse.
The yard in back—tall with dandelions tilting
in a shimmer of warm wind—hums with bees
that bumble on dull pollen-fluffy thighs
and blurring wings back and forth
to a hive hung like the moon in woods behind us.

Higher on the hill, the steady sound of traffic,
and below, the bursting of waves white against black rocks
rises muffled through wild vines and roses
blossoming between us and a sheer fall to the sea,
the two sounds, at that distance, hard to distinguish.

Watching from the windows, our wives,
still strangers, crowd words about the children
into the hopeless silence of neat rooms
where they are trapped and helpless. Our daughters
trade their toys and blows, shyly, with clumsy hands.

We drink and talk as drunken bees
stumble among the yellow sunlit crowns of wild flowers

sprung up in your absence, all but hidden
by June grass I haven't cut yet in July.

By dusk we are quiet, easy with each other,
still among the drowsy pollenated blossoms
abandoned by the bees at last, moonlit, slowly
closing in the dim light at our feet.

WITH MY WIFE BESIDE THE WASHOUGAL RIVER, STILL STRANDED DURING THE FIFTH WEEK OF THE AIRLINES' STRIKE

For Glenn

All day now I've been restless,
camera in hand, waiting
    while the day burns slowly clear
    and wishing I could say just what I want
of you.

This is frightening, to be so far
from how we live or want
    to live. The weeks take
    my desire to think
    away. We came

to see the friends
we only write all year, and spoke
    of how we show our age
    by saying they show theirs,
    laughed

but could not sleep. The sky
is clear now and your face is buried
    in sleep . . . Our friends are gone.
    Remember one, his photographs
    of stone?

PLAYING UNTIL DARK

Spiralling down out of the Guggenheim,
our daughter packed on my back and giddy still
from her first encounter with the colors
of Chagall, whirling in the eye
of Wright's great twister, we venture past
Good Humor men and into Central Park.

Here bums and tourists, the wealthy's colored nursemaids
free of Harlem until dark, and men retired
from everything are gathered on benches
with fallen leaves.

We are tired too, and come here to forget
what time it is and where we are. The child
is our only innocence, and here this afternoon
on the dry grass of a park, we play at being young
while she believes us.
                              Above and behind us
On a boulder half-hidden by trees,
a man on his haunches squats to photograph
a friend who masturbates. His picture
will include us at a distance, playing in the park.
He has made us strangers to ourselves
and strangers to our child in the silence
that has stopped our game. We move on,
and trees conceal their figures on the stone.

Beyond the lined-up benches, we take a path
descending to a lake. All around are nurses,

families picnicking, men asleep with newspapers
and women sitting near them, alone, staring
beyond their children and each other
into those waters of their world
where sullen swans bask, adrift
in the breakage of their own reflections.

CHECKING IN

at 1 a.m., dead tired,
I watch two strangers
carry out a third
across their shoulders,
stiff as a board.

In the step-down lobby,
two whores and a jealous queer
ignore the body
as its eyes open to stare
at me, and these roses for my lady.

An elevator grinds me up
to 3. Stepping off
I breathe again and stop
to check directions: Snuff
and canned spaghetti smells, pop

bottles along a hall
of dead wallpaper flowers. The slick carpet
creaks along the narrow darkness full
of doors locked on regret,
sneak-thieves, and the wounded who can crawl.

SUMMER OF MORNING GLORIES

Coming back from a childhood creek
on an unlit whirring bike at night
and dizzy with the effort on a hill,
I watch the carlights fan out over trees
dying slowly of massive flowering vines
and turn off on the roadside grass,
glad to rest.
       The cars, like insects,
take the crest and speed past in the dark,
leaving me—a child again, in awe of power
and the driver's solitude—to speculate about
the sharp sound of the crickets' dark machine
or fireflies, like floating stars, rising
from the woods, the road,
and even from the weeds that hold our home.

JENNIFER BY MOONLIGHT

A cricket with a short circuit
whirs in grass behind a stone.

The dark electric sound
seems to shine,

attracting our daughter with her
mouthful of moth-wings

toward the porch's edge
where she teeters

on her hands and knees, inarticulate,
and stares.

When a second cricket sizzles
like a star

dunked in a dipper,
she giggles first,

then jabbers at the moon perched
on our Ford.

Carelessly it spills its light
like milk across the yard.

Absorbed
in what she cannot comprehend,

our speechless lady pouts,
vexed

by this brief innocence
of crickets singing and the moon.

FROM THE FIRST AND LASTING DREAM

As I hear crickets threaten from the dark
beyond our window, and watch the moon's old hunt
among sharp branches, my wife curls
in her own deep warmth and stillness.

The car is ours, the house well on its way
to being ours. Whatever ruins memory
has ruined mine: These woods have no beasts left,
my life no fairytales I can forget.

There is a train that sometimes comes
to shake these woods, a loud and prying iron worm
whose windowed belly glows with fetal heads.
Once I dreamed of trains, and how the distance
changes, but worry now: What if the child wakes?
Or cannot wake?
                              Chilled in the silent instant,
I see the small, lit, moonstunned form.

I wake my wife who gently moves now
out of sleeping innocence
and shapes to me, conforms,
admitting deeply the proud surge
that must come with death's urgency
through every generation of desire.

Slowly, Lord, and surely, from the first
and lasting dream shall issue all
our sudden lives, shaped of flesh
conceived in loss, and riven by desire.

THE STORM

1

My father was a skeptic
but a farmer. He believed
in impossibility—
                    waiting
for the Gulf Coast's holocaustal hurricanes,
he'd cut the earth
and seed each fresh wound
with a row of curses,
ram the tractor into gear
and tear his land apart
to put it back together, me beside him
watching, my memory planted
with each season's violent crop, ripening
as each acre ripened.

2

                    This was near
the Everglades fifteen years ago
while I was child learning to live
from a man learning to die.
His life: the steady green profusion
of hot leaves devouring air and light,
sucking rain dark under wide steaming fields
with underground acres of tendrilous roots,

a pale brutal ferocity spreading its strength,
unthinking and gradual.

3
                              Mondays, coughing blood
in handkerchiefs he buried in his fields,
he'd disappear, the high pitched jingle
of a tailgate chain following
toward Colored Town. There he'd bail
his fieldhands out of jail, tallying
that cost against their wages.
He'd disappear, leaving me to stare
at walls the early darkness hid.
                              I'd hear
my mother tossing into sleep, and often woke
at dawn from dreaming of her stifled moans
and turned my pillow over to protect her
from my tears. Then, watching palms
fixed against my window dawn,
I'd wonder what was wrong
and sleep again.

4
                              There was great preparation
before storms. When 48 hour warnings came
he'd hire triple crews at doubled wages,
Puerto Ricans, Negroes, Whites, men
and their wives, truckloads of workers
laughing at first and singing, then anxious
as the thick sky's clouds bulged downward
through the darkness, truckload after truckload
raising dust from each storm-colored road.
He did what could be done against disaster:

Every crop that could be picked was picked
—tomatoes, eggplants, corn or gladiolus,
watermelons—everything ripe enough
to save.
        As I grew old enough
to help, he let me. I bent down
through the hours of song and through the sting
of rain, picked on through the hour of hush
before the wind, excited by the lull
as others whispered, "It's getting time
to stop, it's time to go."
                Then the wind
would start, and then the leaves belly-up,
revealing each green bulge left to the storm.
As distant trucks coughed to life,
"It's time to go!" And large clear drops
like fear fell, chilling our shocked skins.

5
At home our grass was flattened by the wind.
The ancient palms in front arched and creaked,
fronds flinging like the tails of rushing horses.
The boarded house crouched like a cat.
Wind held my door closed till father helped.
Then, pressed against the truck's cold length
and awkward, we crept past the garage to the backyard.
Before we hid in the house, we'd take a leak
and watch wind make it spray for twenty feet.

6
This is the close time of candles, of windows
black with boards, their cracks blackened by the sky,
when windows are opened to keep the house

from exploding, and even his laughter is silence,
trapped in the dim fragile rooms of our home.
In this last longest storm, I am the candle-carrier,
checking every door and window in those rooms
the storm won't let us use. By candlelight
I see rain flicker on the bedroom floors
and I roll up rugs as coconuts like cannonballs
clatter on the street. I bring us blankets,
pillows, sheets, and secret handkerchiefs
for him.
              At night we sleep in the depths
of the house and I dream of my father, coughing.
His crops are ripe around him, tall and still.
Behind his back the sun widens and blinds me
as he coughs and crouches, coughing again.
Trying to scream, I am dumb.
                          I see his gladiolus
dying, the wreckage of 10,000 blossoms floating,
wide useless blossoms, ripe and flimsy,
drowning in the armpit deep floodwater
of flower-shining lakes. The storm
has flushed out cottonmouths
and alligators, leaving coons to starve on stumps
and cypress knees or feed from the bobbing carcasses
of rattlesnakes and rabbits, their long black hands
meticulously waking the smooth surface
of a sky pierced, row on row, by phalanxes
of swordlike stalks, the broken harvest
of my father's curses.
              And as these waters sink,
I come with him although he cannot see me
to slit the throats of pigs, bloated and blacksnouted,
their lips soaked back from white gums

and stained tusks. When the corpses
will not bleed I stand and watch his anger rip
while my blade, thick with gore,
hangs still and helpless. The stench
of vegetables and flesh is rotten all around us.

He crouches against the sun. Above me
his black shoulders heave. One hand is full of light.
The other hand extends toward me from darkness, gently,
turns away my face and lifts my chin.
I cannot scream, my tongue is dead with fear.
I cannot see his face.
                              Lightning
blinds the room: the storm is over
and I wake.

7
            Father, your farm is in the hands
of strangers now and I, a stranger,
waken in strange rooms filled with your presence
as a sky after lightning is still filled
with the scent of light. Faced with glass,
dismembered by its seams, I see you
gaze at herons on a mudflat at sunset.
For years your shape's been paralyzed
among palmettoes' silhouettes,
and now you cough—tossing water
like a shower of fire,
a single heron stretches into flight

and through the burning veil of flashing wings
I see you kneel at last.

The living dark curls up around your back
and you are gone, the dark rising around you
as you bend to plant your blood.

But father, O father,
what silence.